MW01618277

TURKEYTON TOWN

BY D. MELHOFF

ILLUSTRATED BY ARIANE ELSAMMAK

All characters and incidents in this book are fictitious and any resemblance to actual persons, turkeys, or foxes, living or dead, is purely coincidental.

First published by Bellwoods Publishing

First paperback edition

ISBN 978-0992133146

Illustrated by Ariane Elsammak

Book design by Bryce Kirk

www.dmelhoff.com

FACT

Eating a turkey's a mean thing to do,
But if you don't eat *it*, it might just eat *you*.

Murky the turkey stood silent and still,
Staring *straight* in the eyes of the human he killed.
A butcher's knife, glinting, still clutched in his claw,
Dripped sticky red drops from its jaggedy jaw.

Murky looked over at two other birds:
One Lurky, one Quirky. Both lost for words.
"Let's go," muttered Murky. "We can't miss the feast.
Grab his arms, drag his legs—
He won't mind, he's deceased."

The bird had a point; the human was dead
(if he wasn't, then *they* would be butchered instead).
So Murky and Lurky both moved for the coop,
while Quirky just gawked.
Quite out of the loop.

When Quirky was hatched in his thatched mother's nest,
They knew he was different from all of the rest.
He was peaceful and kind and enjoyed relaxation,
And had *no* known plans for world domination.

He spoke not a word, having nothing to say,
And felt clucking and gobbles were much too cliché.
So mostly, like now, he escorted his brothers
In silence, avoiding discussions with others.

Together the brothers arrived
at their nests, where they sat,
one by one, with their dead farmer guest.
Then WOOSH!
The seats plunged with each turkey on top—
Like trapdoors, they were gone
down a bottomless drop.

WELCOME
TO
Turkeyton Town

A hundred feet under the farm and the coop,
The turkey bros landed with three windy swoops.
They'd come to a cavern called Turkeyton Town:
A whole *world* where turkeys ruled underground!

Beaks & Bangs
GOBBLE

Their nests were all tucked in the catacomb domes,
With bedrooms, decks, pantries—fully loaded like homes!
There were gardens and markets and feather salons,
And schools! Ice rinks! Statues that glowed golden bronze!

Old Murky led Lurky and Quirky along,
Through tunnels and taverns and tight turkey throngs,
'Til they came to a kitchen where mountains of food
Were baking and boiling and being fondued.

But this feast was no regular Thanksgiving feast,
For inside their ovens cooked no bird nor beast;
But rather, all seasoned with parsley and cumin,
Cooked dozens of juicy, plump, porky humans.

S
P

Meanwhile...

Above, in a forest at some frozen spot,
Were four scrawny foxes around a stone pot.
All ragged and starving, their spirits were low,
And their eyes shone hot hatred that blazed through the snow.

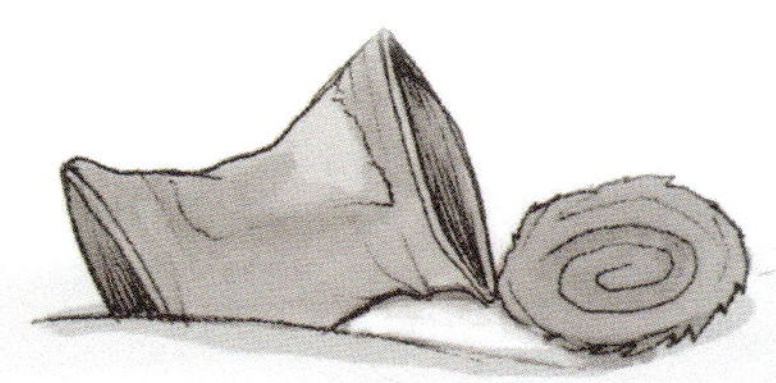

"Let's go," coughed one fox as he slunk to his feet,
"Get yer bushy ends up and let's find some meat."
"Meat?" laughed another. "Have you gone insane?
Why not caviar too? With expensive champagne?"

"QUIET!" the largest fox cried like a gun.
"Hurry up—don't forget I'm still Fox Number One!"
So each wrapped a tattered red scarf 'round his neck,
Then they stumbled and wheezed down a long, frosty trek.

After hours of searching and fighting the breeze,
They spotted a farm and a coop through the trees.
All over were turkeys—all through the yard—
Some washing,
some marching,
and some standing guard.

The foxes drooled buckets—they'd hit the grand prize!
So close to wings, drumsticks, and fat juicy thighs!
Yet since they were clever and cunning and slick,
They thought up plans fast for a terrible trick.

While the turkeys weren't watching, they snuck tippy-toed
To the farmer's old house and dressed up in his clothes.

Then before they departed, sly Fox Number One
Snatched the farmer's long gun and said, "This should be fun..."

So the four “farmers” strolled to the edge of the yard,
And then tapped on the backs of the turkeys on guard.
The lookouts ERUPTED like high-pitched alarms,
And assembled a flock from all over the farm.

They swarmed 'round the farmers, who held up their hands
(Surrendering now was just part of the plan),
Then the birds took them captive and led like police
Through the coop, down the nests to their marvelous feast.

Below the birds gathered, prepared for their meal—
Every bird except Quirky (who hates this ordeal).
He doesn't eat meat, he doesn't chew bones,
So he hides in the caves every year, all alone.

The last of the turkeys paraded inside,
And they brought in the foxes—all four still disguised.
Then they marched to the kitchen and cranked up the stoves,
When, like FIREWORKS, the foxes burst from their clothes!

The guards grabbed their knives, but the foxes just smiled
And flexed their clawed fingers, all sharpened and riled.
They whipped out their rifle and aimed left and right,
And the turkeys collapsed and surrendered the fight.

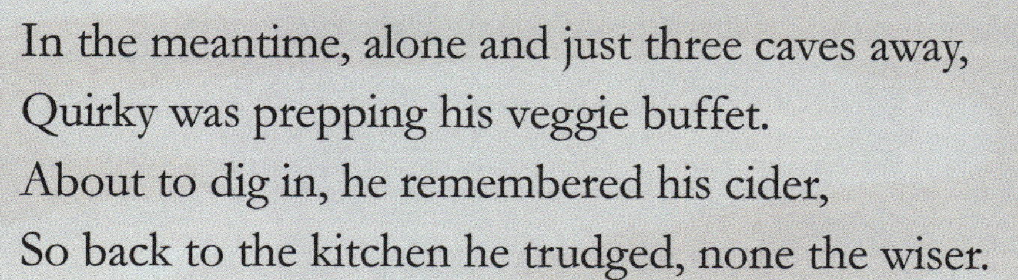

In the meantime, alone and just three caves away,
Quirky was prepping his veggie buffet.
About to dig in, he remembered his cider,
So back to the kitchen he trudged, none the wiser.

When Quirky arrived at the outskirts of town,
He was *stunned* by the sight of the scene all around.
The turkeys were shackled and queued to be stew,
And Quirky just froze. *No clue* what to do.

He saw the four foxes all stuffing their faces,
And old farmer clothes (by the door of all places).
He had an idea, though the stakes were sky high—
Could it rescue the town?
If so, worth a try.

He ducked in the kitchen and crouched near the door,
Then stealthily swiped the old clothes from the floor.
The foxes, all four of them laughing and cheering,
Never noticed their shirts or their gun disappearing.

Suddenly, the oven lights blinked 405—
Time came for the turkeys to all roast alive!
The foxes slunk closer and flashed their white fangs,
When all of a sudden boomed three thunderous BANGS!

The birds whipped directions so fast that they spun
To see *some figure* clutching the farmer's long gun.
It wobbled through smoke like a man with wood legs—
The turkeys, astonished, laid on-the-spot eggs.

This figure was costumed in plaid farmer clothes:
The pants hiked too high and the sleeves slung too low.
A white cotton beard dangled loose by his cheeks,
And his nose looked a lot like a sharp turkey beak.

The fox brothers' jaws all dropped open in shock,
While the farmer aimed up the long gun 12 o'clock…
Yet a gleam in his pupil said 'don't pull the trigger';
Killing is killing. He could choose to be bigger.

ngs
GOBBLE

But that pause was enough to let Fox Number One
Come pouncing and knock back both farmer and gun.
In a colorful whirlwind of orange, white, and brown,
GUNSHOT BLASTS banged and clanged through Turkeyton Town.

Smoke settled, dust floated in soft spun designs;
The farmer looked up to see harm of all kinds.
The kitchen was ruined, the feast was destroyed,
But the turkeys had lived. He relaxed, overjoyed.

Meanwhile, Murky stood silent and still,
Staring *straight* in the eyes of the foxes he killed.
The farmer's gun, smoking, still clutched in his claws
Had ended the carnage with four lightning draws.

Then Murky turned slowly and looked at the birds;
The whole town of turkeys awaited his words.
"We're wrecked," announced Murky. "They've ruined our feast.
They're bony, we're starving—fox *won't* do the least!"

A couple feet back, Quirky raised from his daze;
He'd saved the whole town, but where was the praise?
Then came a strange sight—why, his eyes *must* be fooling.
Why were the turkeys all watching him? Drooling?

HAPPY THANKSGIVING

A few hours later, the birds sat together,
All chatting and passing food feather-to-feather.
The feast had been ruined, but here was a soup
Where little meat chunks bobbed around in each scoop.

The turkeys gave thanks for still being around,
As they ladled their dishes and passed them on down.
And in this orange broth floated bits by the gallons,
As well as two unnoticed, innocent talons.

Dear Reader:

Do you ever feel guilty about eating turkey? Don't.

These birds, as you are now aware, are some of the cruelest beasts to roam the planet. The next time one of them comes across your plate, please remember the tragedy of Quirky and do your best to devour every bite.

Also, finish your vegetables.

D. MELHOFF

D. Melhoff is best known for his adult horror novels; however, he also enjoys terrifying younger audiences from time to time. For more of Melhoff's illustrated tales, visit www.dmelhoff.com.

Made in the USA
Lexington, KY
07 November 2014